CW01623432

FOOTPRINTS IN THE SNOW

BY

JACKIE HUCK

Copyright © Jackie Huck, 2017

All rights reserved. No part of this book may be copied, reproduced, stored in a retrieval system or transmitted, in any form or by any electronic or mechanical means without the prior permission of the copyright owner.

Cover image supplied by Jackie Huck

Typeset by: 2QT Limited, Publishing

ISBN 978-1-912014-17-0
Printed and bound by: TJ International LTD

INTRODUCTION TO

'FOOTPRINTS IN THE SNOW'

I started writing an annual poem to put in my Christmas cards in the mid 1970's. At first handwritten and sent only to a few people. As modern home technology improved, and it became easier to print, most people received a 'poem card'. In the early part of the century I decided to arrange these poems into small booklets. The first effort of just a few pages, was 'Under an Eagle's Wing' this later developed into 'Footprints in the Snow' followed a few years later by 'The Three Trees'.

For the first time I have collected all the Christmas Card poems into one book, adding other poems written for concerts and different occasions. The result is this enlarged Christmas collection.

Christmas means many things to many people. It evokes a host of memories, the happy and the sad. Time and age change our attitudes to the festive season, and makes us approach Christmas in different ways.

The poems reflect this variety of emotions, and since they were written over a time scale spanning forty years, my own life and the changing world around, are at times reflected in the poems.

A number of the poems have a religious theme, because we sometimes forget that Christmas means 'Christ's Mass' and Christmas is to celebrate the birth of Jesus. I have found over the years a number of varying approaches to the Christmas story.

In Great Britain Christmas is always associated with winter, and is especially important when one lives in the countryside, with the problems this time of year inflicts on rural communities. It also adds an extra level of beauty, these thoughts are reflected in the winter poems.

But life is fun, and to laugh is important, there's a lot of fun to be found amongst the collection.

I considered calling the collection 'A Christmas Bundle' for that's what it is, but settled for one of the original titles 'Footprints in the Snow' which is reflected in the first poem. In this poem Jesus leaves his footprints, but we all leave our footprints not necessarily in the snow, but in the life we lead.

~ Contents ~

FOOTPRINTS IN THE SNOW

He gave us joy, he gave us love,
He gave us everything,
Snowflakes in the winter,
Raindrops in the spring,
He showed us how to live our lives
He taught us how to grow,
Now it's time to follow
His Footprints in the Snow.

Hearts are filled with happiness
When Santa comes to call,
There's turkey in the oven,
Holly in the hall,
Christmas trees are decked with light
There's stars and mistletoe,
All because a special child,
Left Footprints in the Snow.

Then came the day, time stood still,
All the world grew dark,
Hearts were filled with sorrow
Dogs forgot to bark,
They thought that they had finished him
How little did they know,
His truth is written in the stars,
His footprints fill the Snow.

All round the world this story's told
Wherever Christians are,
Of Wise Men and Three Shepherds,
Angels and a Star,
A child who came at Christmas-time
To set the earth a-glow,
To leave us dreams and promises,
And Footprints in the Snow.

THE LO....N..GGGGG.... CHRISTMAS

Christmas starts in August,
with the first cards on the shelves,
followed rapidly by plastic balls,
lights and grinning elves.

The first week in September the
letter box is jammed,
with all those charity brochures,
which pleadingly demand
your money for the needy,
'look at all our gifts within,'
and it makes you feel a rotter,
if you chuck them in the bin.

The first week in October,
and we think of foreign post,
stock-up on cranberry sauce and pickles
and that sherry for the toast.

Come November starts the gallop,
round the hankies and the socks,
computer games and tokens,
and 'smellies' by the box.

Then at last you reach December,
in a panic and a sweat,
POST EARLY!! scream the posters,
and in case you might forget
they're counting down the shopping days,
and you're working through your list,
while each post brings fond greetings,
from the people that you've missed!

So it finally reaches Christmas,
all your presents have been sent,
you've bought the turkey and the stuffing,
you're appalled at what you've spent.
Then the festive bells are ringing,
there's carol singers at the door,
the shops are barred and shuttered,
you can't buy any more.

You're full with Christmas pudding,
the crackers have been pulled,
the dogs sicked back his dinner,
and you're heads like wine that's mulled!
Gran's moaning at the telly,
the kids have fallen out,
and you're sitting with the cat,
wondering what it's all about.

But if anybody asks you,
"Was your Christmas good or bad?"
You'll answer, "It was smashing,
The best we've ever had!"

TRIMMING THE TREE

Bring out the box where the bright bells are kept,
safe with the glass and the glister,
that elderly angel who whirls on a thread,
pale and pink-winged like her sister.
The old Woolworths baubles we bought long ago,
treasured as jewels from The Tower,
cotton-wool snow and that little fat elf
who swings from a shimmering flower.

I've bought chocolate Santa's, (we ate all last year
along with the reindeers and holly),
and shinny net-fairies that spin all the day,
gold garlands will look rather jolly.
I've tossed twisted tinsel as threads of fine ice,
and added a rolly-poll clown,
while right at the top, winks the star father shaped,
the tree once more wears her spiked crown.

But each little thing that I add to the tree
brings a memory of Christmas's past,
time hurries by as the garlands grow dim
years seem to tumble so fast.
Gleam Christmas lights trimmed round our tree
this is your moment to shine,
in remembrance of Him who brought joy to the world,
His love hold your dear ones and mine.

~ THE CHRISTMAS ROSE ~

When winter skies are grey with rain
and it feels like the sun will not smile again.
When the leaves are old with nothing new,
the Christmas Rose comes gleaming through.

A radiant light lit a manger bed
bringing rays of hope, when hope seemed dead,
so the Christmas Rose lights the winter brown
as the purest gems in The Lord's own crown.

So, if your heart feels dull and sad,
when the frost is keen and the gales are bad,
down in a stable pure and new,
let The Christmas Rose shine for you.

LADY WINTER

Lady Winter brilliant in your bridal gown,
Kissing slates, bringing radiance to the town,
Draping braid on branches bare as bone.
You spin a beauty especially your own.

Trimming fences with a crystal layer,
The morning sun in orange flare
Sends rainbow patterns dancing over snow,
Painting magic patterns in your icy glow.

Lady Winter shimmering in your party dress
A storm-winged herald come to bless,
While Christmas trees and silver bells
Ring tidings through the snow-shot fells.

Lady Winter, weeping in your widows weeds,
Your dying days sow the seeds
Of hope, as life is trembling ready for the spring
When green awakes, and birds returning, sing!

Lady Winter in your spiral round,
Coating windows, stroking silver on the ground,
Bewitching Mistress, transient stepping stone,
You smile and make the world your own.

IT'S THE THOUGHT THAT COUNTS

At this festive time, when everyone is busy sorting out cards and presents, I always think back to one of my elderly aunts. She has long departed to her 'elderly aunt cloud', but I see her still.

She lived with my uncle, a gentle, down-trodden little man, in a gloomy house in Ashton. She was as miserable as she was frugal, and 'Scrooge' (before his transformation) would have called her a friend. The electric lights were never allowed on until the sky had lost all its brightness. Even on the darkest winter day, the only light in the house came from the few coals, on the meagre fire. To make the room even darker, a large aspidistra filled the window-sill.

Whatever Mum found to talk about on our weekly visits, I have no idea. I would amuse myself with Uncle's fingers, which on one hand were permanently pressed flat against his roughened palm. I would work diligently, pulling the fingers up-right, only for them to rebound back immediately.

Shortly before Christmas each year, we would pay our ritual Christmas visit, with a card and a pair of socks for uncle, and a scarf or gloves for aunty. The room would be unchanged. Aunty didn't believe in Christmas trees or decorations, and instead of standing the cards up on the mantelpiece, she would press them into a neat, thin pile.

Her festive cheer consisted of a couple of chocolate biscuits, and perhaps an extra sandwich. I was therefore flabbergasted when one Christmas, towards the end of her life, she pressed a small, flat package into my palm, with the words, "just a little something for Christmas."

I nearly chocked on a crust with shock, but thanked her dutifully, intrigued to know what she had given me.

I somehow retained my curiosity until Christmas morning, when the family gathered for the traditional 'present opening'. Slowly I opened the brown paper parcel, to reveal a packet of nylon stockings. To gales of laughter, the white-card packaging was read: 'A Free Gift From Stork Margarine'!

A TEDDY BEAR'S ARMS

Christmas dreams when I was a child
Began with a golden bear,
        Who growled, "Hallo" one Christmas Eve
        As Santa crept up the stair,
Eye's tight closed, I would not look,
Or the magic would slip away,
        But the paper parcels crackled
        How I longed for the coming day,
And with the kiss of morning
Which held a thousand charms,
        I remember that early Christmas
        As I lay in a teddy-bear's arms.

Those days of painted pictures
As Christmas came and went,
        Paper-chains to lick and stick,
        A half-crown to be spent,
Chestnuts smoking at the fire,
A fairy on the tree
        Who was brought out each December,
        And had lived as long as me.
A new doll or a spinning top,
Turkey and mince pies,
        But nothing ever matched the love
        I saw in a teddy-bear's eyes.

School Concerts and the Annual Play,
One year I was a king,
    Arrayed in velvet curtains
    My verse to proudly sing,
Be-jewelled and crowned with cardboard,
With parents to applaud,
    We laid gifts round the manger
    And hailed the new born Lord,
Songs to waken memories,
Carols to beguile,
    But I think back to that Christmas
    And the joy in a teddy-bear's smile.

He's seen a host of years since then
His golden fur's worn thin,
    His loving smile has been kissed away
    Leaving a faded grin.
He growls no more, his head is loose,
His gold has turned to brown,
    He's left alone, a forgotten toy
    Who wears a lonely frown -
But when each year the memories stir,
It's then I remember the charms,
    I found that Christmas long ago,
    As I lay in a teddy-bear's arms.

~ ALONE ~

It's Christmas Day, she's all alone,
No knock on the door, no voice on the phone,
No family gathering with laughter to share,
Just rain on the window, but nobody's there.

The clock strokes the hours,
        Her fire flickers low,
As memories flash back
        In the ember's faint glow,
Echoes of carols
        Sang round a tree,
A child clutching presents;
        A babe on her knee.

Turkeys that sizzled,
        Crackling of pork,
White sauce and plum pudding,
        The pop! Of a cork.
Games round a parlour,
        Neighbours to call:
Now dusty shadows,
        Wind up the hall.

Old fingers turn pages of black and white snaps,
With girls in print-pinnies, boys in flat caps.

She looks at a girl with youth aglow -
sighs and wonders -
    "Where did she go?"

"CAN'T COOK! WON'T COOK! ESPECIALLY CHRISTMAS DINNER"

I think we'll start with melon, I know I can't burn that
It might end up a funny shape, with one end thin, one fat,
But I'll dress it with a tin of fruit, and pop a cherry on the top -
Oh - I might just get a tin of soup, from the local shop.

I'll buy a pre-cooked chicken, and a jar of apple sauce,
Then a tin of new potatoes, and a tin of peas of-course,
I better get some Brussels sprouts, I think they sell them frozen,
And a great big blob of stuffing, to round off what I've chosen.

I've brought a luxury Christmas pudding, from the
Marks and Spencer's range,
And we'll have a tin of white sauce
instead of custard for a change,
We'll finish off with 'After Eights',
and wine to toast The Queen,
It'll be the finest spread of food my tables ever seen.

So as you slave for ages, expanding sweat and power -
Remember that my banquet, took just half an hour.

THE STORY THE FAIRY TOLD

Santa, a reindeer, a green elf and me
brought from our boxes to hang on the tree,
I am the fairy with bright wings to fly,
the reindeer bears Santa's sleigh through the sky,
the elf is his helper who sorts all the toys,
that come down the chimney's for good girls and boys.

But, who are these figures, not jolly at all
men in long robes, and a maid in a shawl?
There's cattle, and sheep, and a pile of old hay,
more important than us, I heard someone say!

They've been placed on the table, in pride of place,
it really won't do, it's such a disgrace,
everyone knows it's our time of year,
with presents, and turkey, and toasts of 'Good Cheer'.

Now in the centre a manger's appeared,
getting all the attention, (just as I feared),
there is a tiny babe nestled within -
and it turns out that Christmas,
is all about Him!

~ "IT'S THE MISSING YOU" ~

It's the missing you, and you, and you -
Christmas brings you nearer,
I see you clearer than in spring.
        As I trim the tree
        I see your collective smiles,
        Carols echo with your song,
        Now silent.
Even Santa with his well-filled sack,
Cannot bring you back,
I say the old familiar words,
        Laugh, pull crackers, sing -
        But, I know that I am blest
        You are the best in me,
And I will raise my glass
To you,
        and you,
                and you –

A SHOEBOX FOR CHRISTMAS

What would you put in a shoebox?
        To brighten a child's Christmas Day,
A child who has little or nothing,
        Who lives in a land far away.

A small teddy-bear with a ribbon,
A woollen-thread smile and pale hair,
Who will be a new friend in the darkness,
When it feels that the world doesn't care.
Perhaps coloured crayons and paper
To cheer up a life that is drab,
In a little shoebox with plain treasures,
Which divide the "have not's" from the "have."

So what will I put in my shoebox
To send to this unknown child?
Along with the toys and the chocolates,
Maybe a letter of hope I've compiled -
"That even though we might be strangers,
My prayer and my wish is sincere,
That the peace that our Lord brought at Christmas,
Brings you comfort and love all the year.

(Operation Christmas Child sends shoeboxes of gifts to needy children in Kosovo, Albania, Romania, Ukraine and Poland)

THE CUMBRIAN DONKEY

The wind blew chill on the fells that night,
Mountain peaks dusted white,
A stony track through the twisting vale,
The man was strong, the woman pale,
Far to go, the journey long,
To the steady clip of a hoof-beat song,
As the Cumbrian donkey plodded on

Church bells pealed from a distant tower,
As a clock proclaimed the midnight hour,
Christmas stole through the sleeping earth,
With simple joy for a baby's birth,
But the rugged path lay far ahead,
Leading on to a cattle shed,
A lonely road, to a wondrous day
As the Cumbrian donkey found his way.

Dawn came creeping of shallow gold,
The day was young, the world was old,
Tired of waiting for grains of hope
Bourne by hooves down a winding slope.
A new child cried on the morning air,
But warm in his stable without a care,
Dreaming dreams of the great unknown
The Cumbrian donkey had reached his home.

IMAGES OF WINTER

Winter and the clouds have cracked
emptying naked whiteness on the fells,
rimming blue-grey lakes,
draping elephant-shaped hills,
filling fractured valleys and bony crags.

Stone walls fork in crazy patterns
black ink scrawled through snow,
and all is shining ice, diamond-like,
winking, as a stolen sun
dances falsely over chiselled crests.

Fleshless trees, wait against
a pale-pink picture-postcard sky,
and sleeping stalk and bush bend
beneath a weight of white.

Whilst we, who would command the moon
and visit stars
stand powerless,
as winter subjugates us all!

COMING HOME FOR CHRISTMAS (2009)

He's coming home for Christmas
from grim Afghanistan,
they sent him out a soldier boy
he's coming home a man.
He's trudged through dusty townships
ready with his gun,
thinking of his girl friend
and that letter from his mum.
He's fought in wretched outposts
where a rabbit couldn't thrive,
had bullets whistle passed his head
and walked away alive.
He's shared a laugh and story
with his mates, and learnt to care
for the pal who guards his back,
then one day he's not there.
He's tried to help the locals,
and some of them's okay,
but you never know when one will turn
and blow your brains away.

So, he's cursed 'the ***** politicians'
and he's cursed 'the ***** war!"
but after all a soldier
doesn't question what it's for,
he just tries to do his duty,
learns to cope with threat and fear,
and dreams about his home
and the ones that he holds dear.
So, he's coming home for Christmas,
where the silent crowds will show,
tribute to a soldier
and the man they'll never know.

~ SCROOGE ~

(With thanks to Charles Dickens for 'A Christmas Carol', surely the best Christmas book ever.)

Marley was dead, let there be no mistake,
As dead as a skewer, stabbed in a steak,
Scrooge carried on making money in piles,
With no place in his heart for pity or smiles.
Bob Cratchit his Clerk, fingers stiff from the cold
Worked at his books, as the new year grew old,
As Christmas approached, a time of good cheer,
"Humbug!" shouted Scrooge,
"I'll have none of that here."

As Scrooge reached his door that bleak Christmas Eve,
He started with fear, and could not believe
His eyes, as he looked at his knocker and saw
Old Marley's face, with his death-bandaged jaw,
Then through the dark as Scrooge suppered alone,
Came a clanging of chains, a scream and a groan
As Marley appeared with his shackles of shame,
"If you don't change your ways Scrooge,
you'll end up the same!"

"Three Spirits will haunt you, the first one will come
With darkness tomorrow as the Church Bell tolls one,
The second the next night at the same hour
You cannot escape them they have immense power,
Expect the third as the midnight stroke fades
Your one chance for redemption, lies in these shades.
So, dragging his chains Marley slid out of sight
To continue his endless trudge, night after night.

The bell echoed 'One' through the chill of his room,
As the bed-curtains opened and out of the gloom
A spectre appeared and bore Scrooge away
Back to his past, down a dismal highway,
To a lonely child, and a sister he lost,
To a growing man who cared only for cost,
And Scrooge wept tears for a Christmas song
As he traced his life, as it all went wrong.

Woken from sleep. "Know Me!" came a cry,
His room was transformed with food piled high,
As The Ghost of the Present filled the night with his glow,
Scrooge touched his robe, off they did go
To see Cratchit's family rejoicing and glad,
Filled with love for each other with the little they had
Shared round, and the glory of Christmas shone bright,
As Scrooge suddenly heard the strokes of Midnight –

And the Ghost of the Future stood hooded as death,
"I fear you more than the others,"
gasped Scrooge as his breath
Hung in the air, but if the Ghost heard
The phantom just pointed and spoke not a word
As he showed him a cruel world
where no-one would care
That an embittered miser was no longer there,
Unloved and forgotten, alone at the last
Just a neglected headstone, to show he had passed.

"No Spirit! I vow I will change!
You will see!
The Spirits all three, shall strive within me,
I will honour each Christmas, and keep it all year,
Just give me a chance! Oh Spirit, please hear!"

And true to his word Scrooge became a good man,
As good a friend and a master as any man can,
He learnt how to laugh and his love to impart,
And the blessings of Christmas burned in his heart.

THE PANTOMIME PIG

He fancied they'd cast him as King or a hero,
Or a Prince with a rapier and velvet bolero,
He would make a fine Wizard, with pointed top hat,
With a vast range of spells, and of-course a black cat.

Perhaps as Dandeni or Buttons he'd shine,
Or as Grumpy the dwarf on his way from the mine,
In fact in most parts he knew he'd be big,
But the teacher has made him,
        The Pantomime Pig!

As Dick Whittington's cat he'd have made a fine show,
Or as poor old Jack's Beanstalk, he'd have shown
        how to grow.
As the blackest of villains he'd have made the crowd
boo!!
As a cute dancing cow, he'd have known how to moo.

What a marvellous Aladdin with Lamp he'd have made,
As Red Riding Hood's wolf he'd have made her afraid,
He'd have cut such a dash in a cloak or a wig,
But the teacher has made him,
        The Pantomime Pig.

He's learning to squeal; she won't let him sing,
And he's only got grunts, not a script like the King!
He's tried on his costume, he thinks he looks daft,
He's not even a sword or a feather to waft.

He quite likes his trotters and cute curly tail
But he'd much have preferred a black suit of mail,
He'd have swung just like Tarzan clad in a fig,
    But teacher insisted,
    "YOU'RE PANTOMIME PIG!!"

But - come the performance,
    Those in the know,
    Said, "The Pantomime Pig,
    Was the star of The Show!"

THE ANGEL WHO MISSED CHRISTMAS DAY

When the world was awaking from sleep,
When The Shepherds were leaving their sheep,
When the sun's golden ray, heralded the new day,
While over the mountains The Kings sped away,
Then I saw a small light in the sky,
And from out of the clouds came a cry,
"Though I've flown through the night,
Still I've missed the great sight,
Just because I was too far away,
I'm the Angel who missed Christmas Day."

But this Angel was needed elsewhere,
For a million hearts laden with care,
Shed no tears for her fate, out of love she was late,
But the wonder of Christmas for her couldn't wait.
Though the years may go rolling along,
I will still hear that Angel's sweet song,
For we all need the love that is sent from above,
And we all can be thankful and pray,
For the Angel, who missed Christmas Day.

SPARE A THOUGHT IN PASSING

Sing the same old carols, in the same old way,
Send the same old greetings, on each Christmas Day,
But as you open presents,
        beneath your Christmas Tree,
Spare a thought in passing, for the likes of me.

I heard the carols echo
        as I scrambled through the mud,
then lying in a shell-hole fighting
        bowels and blood,
I saw 'me old mate Sammy
        dancing on the wire,
it looked like he was waving
        in-between the riffle fire,
I stared across the broken ground,
        but saw no 'peace on earth',
I only saw a battle field,
        where dead men bruised the turf.
I used to open presents
Beneath a Christmas Tree,
So - spare a thought in passing
        For the likes of me.

I live in Cardboard City,
        the pavement is my bed,
I sleep amongst the rubbish
        with a paper round my head,
perhaps on Christmas morning
        I'll get some soup for free,
so spare a thought in passing
        for the likes of me.

The shells fall in the valley
where the children used to play,
I'm living under plastic
on a hillside far away,
or wandering through the mountains
in the early winter snow,
driven from my ruined house
with no-where left to go.

I'd love to open presents
Beneath your Christmas Tree,
        So - spare a thought in passing
        For the likes of me.

I’m a million hungry bellies,
        I’m a million refugees,
I’m the silent voice of poverty,
        desperation and disease,
I’m the ghost you never think of,
        I’m the voice you never hear,
I’m the shadow in the distance,
        I’m the cry and un-dried tear.
I’ll never open presents
        Beneath a Christmas Tree,
So - spare a thought in passing,
        For the likes of me.

Sing the same old carols, in the same old way,
Send the same old greetings, on each Christmas Day,
But as you open presents,
        beneath your Christmas Tree,
Spare a thought in passing, for the likes of me.

THE CHRISTMAS MOUSE

The family sleeping as Christmas Day
closed its eyes, and slipped away,
the turkey down to the threads of bones,
little left but scraps and scones.
When silently from around the suite,
stole two little eyes on four little feet,
a tiny nose twitched, hunting a crumb,
as the humans slept his time had come,
so through the tinsel, about the house
with such delight sped the Christmas mouse.

He chased a cracker across the floor,
hung on holly which dressed the door,
nibbled a candle into the wick,
and climbed to the top of a glittery stick,
he danced through streamers and golden balls,
sniffed and admired cards on the walls,
swung on a bell to make it ring,
and nosed through presents, toys and bling,
though he popped a balloon, no-one stirred in
the house,
but he jumped in fright, did the Christmas
mouse.

He made a meal from morsels he found,
that the people had left lying around,
sandwich crusts, a snippet of cake,
pieces of pie, and sweet tray bake,
remains of plum pudding, wine and rum,
filled to exploding, having such fun -
'till he felt rather giddy, his head in a spin,
so he pattered away, with a hiccup and grin,
back to his hole hidden deep in the house,
where he snored until dawn,
did the Christmas mouse.

HE SMILES IN THE HAY

The Angels are singing around you tonight,
This dark world of sorrow is filling with light,
All for a baby who smiles in the hay,
A gift from above on this first Christmas Day.

From up on the hills Shepherds answer a call,
They come through the night to an old cattle stall,
They find a baby that smiles in the hay,
A gift from above on this first Christmas Day.

Kings from the East by a star they are led,
They bring gifts of gold to this old cattle shed,
They worship a baby who smiles in the hay,
A gift from above on this first Christmas Day.

****

All over the world still this story is told,
Of shepherds and Angels and gifts made of gold,
All for a baby who smiled in the hay,
A gift for us all on that first Christmas Day.

PAPER WINGS

I remember how you stood
between the other Angels
shuffling sideways, halo wobbling
on its wire,
bumping paper wings, shimmering
in tinsel
and silk curtains.

Brown hair ringed your little face
which shone in expectation,
dimples dancing as your singing
filled the room
with practised chorus, ringing sweet
through rafters,
music soared away.

Proud mothers hunted hankies
mouthing silent prompts, as voices
echoed softly. But my haunting thought
amongst my tears
was for the years to come, when
you would loose your innocence,
and burn your paper wings.

~ SNOWDROPS ~

Chaste maidens, heads bowed in supplication,
veiled nuns, whispering together,
white flashes in the drab,
as winter struggles into spring,
patches peeping from the brown,
cocktail of fallen leaves
dappling the ground.
Some as family groups
huddled in discourse,
lining water banks,
lighting dark walls,
fringing fields,
dainty damsels.
Or in profusion,
massed spectators,
listeners, waiting for a sermon
below God's throne.

~ CHRISTMAS EVE ~

Christmas eve, snow has fallen
all is crisp and white,
through the land children waiting
for Santa in the night.
Bells ring in the Midnight Mass
as Christians hail the day,
when Jesus slept beneath a star
cradled in the hay.

From Bethlehem, to Northern shores
across the timeless seas,
carols swell with simple faith,
carried on the breeze,
and as it has across the years
Christmas shines again,
because a child brought hope and love
that special night He came.

THE SHEPHERD BOY

Come little shepherd boy, out of the blue
heaven has fashioned a memory for you,
close by a stable door, hear a soft cry,
peep little shepherd, no need to be shy.
Three Kings from afar, gathering with gold,
to worship a new child, the prophets foretold,
and there kneels your father, a smile on his face,
beckoned by love, to this holy place,
where a woman and man, nurse a baby who brings
hope to the world, and so many things
spring from these moments, you witness today.
Come little shepherd boy, tip-toe away.

~ THE FAIRY ~

Ho! Ho! Ho! Hee! Hee! Hee!
I am the Fairy on the Christmas Tree.

When Christmas Time is over
They pack me in a box,
With Santa and his Reindeer
    And an elf with sweaty socks!
We all get very cosy
    And then we start to dose,
And I wake up with an elf and a sock
    And a moth-ball up my nose.

Ho! Ho! Ho! Hee! Hee! Hee!
I am the Fairy on the Christmas Tree.

I'm such a busy fairy
    I work the whole year long,
A box that's filled with reindeer
    Let's off an awful pong!!
Last Christmas Santa bought me
    Not tinsel for my hair,
But a shovel and a brush, and a refuse bag
    And Wellingtons to wear.

Ho! Ho! Ho! Hee! Hee! Hee!
I am the Fairy on the Christmas Tree.

In summer it is stuffy,
        The autumn nights are long,
We fill them up with a tale and a laugh
        And a jolly fairy song.
The elf he told a good one
        About the mistletoe,
And who tickled Santa,
        And Santa said, “Ho! Ho!”

Ho! Ho! Ho! Hee! Hee! Hee!
I am the Fairy on the Christmas Tree.

At last it’s time for Christmas
        They stick me on the tree,
And all the elves and other things
        Are looking up at me,
Perhaps you think that’s marvellous
        But really I’m quite hurt,
How would you like twenty elves
        Gazing up your skirt?

Ho! Ho! Ho! Hee! Hee! Hee!
I am the Fairy on the Christmas Tree.

Now pity the poor fairy
        Upon the Christmas Tree,
No-one feeds her turkey
        A hungry fairy she!
No tasty little titbits
        To put inside her tum,
All she gets is a great big twig
        Sticking up her bum!!

Ho! Ho! Ho! Hee! Hee! Hee!
I am the Fairy on the Christmas Tree.

So as you pack your fairy
        Back inside her box,
Don't put her in with a randy elf
        With a pair of sweaty socks,
And as you pass your fairy
        On the tree-top pity her,
She's sitting there with a twig up her bum
        And she's shovelled ---- all year!!

Ho! Ho! Ho! Hee! Hee! Hee!
I am the Fairy on the Christmas Tree.

THE MUSIC OF CHRISTMAS

'God Rest Ye Merry Gentlemen'
wrote someone long ago,
while 'Good old King Wenceslas'
is trudging through the snow,
that 'Little town of Bethlehem'
proclaimed a holy birth,
as 'Angels from the Realms of Glory'
sang of peace on earth.

'I've wondered as I've wandered'
about 'Three Ships' in a line,
we've had 'Jingle Bells' and 'Frosty'
singing 'Mistletoe and Wine',
'Kings of Orient' passed this way,
that very 'First Nowell'
'While Shepherds Watched their Flocks by Night'
is what the carols tell.

Each Christmas ring these gentle tunes,
through concert, church and snow,
we carry them within our hearts,
we learnt them long ago,
they wrap us in remembrance
each note a memory clear,
so - may the well-known Yuletide songs
fill you with joy this year.

~ WINTER WALK ~

Treading old grass,
I pass stone walls, white blotched by time,
moss topped.
Mud marks tractor treads,
as pheasants sprint away.

Today a generous winter sun
picks out the fells.
Wild Boar, distant faded brown,
The Howgills sombre green,
Shap topped by a string of light
beneath approaching cloud,
but Orton Scar smiles with gold.

Wind grips me on the upper fields,
a boggy scramble down begins,
as icy gusts dash through
thin bones of trees.

It’s growing calmer now,
sun dazzles as I clamber without grace
across the stile.
I pick a path through squelching slush,
thankfully no rush, finding stones
on solid ground.

Mole hills and sheep. Nearly down.
I paddle to the final gate,
from there the track leads home.
A final blaze of white, from a failing sun,
before the dying of the light.

THE CHILDREN'S CHRISTMAS LISTS

All over the world as Christmas draws near,
Children are hoping that someone will hear,
Santa or parents, grandad will do,
To buy all those presents, make wishes come true.

****

"Oh, send me a spaceman for Christmas,
The one with antennas that flash,
Equipped with a laser that splutters,
And a stun-gun that goes with a crash!"

"Oh, send me a new doll for Christmas,
The one with the hair that will grow,
With a wiggle she walks, with a giggle she talks,
And she even does things down below."

"Oh, send me some trainers for Christmas,
In the very top fashion designed,
With laces and ridges, and built-in wedge bridges,
A boot and a plimsoll combined."

"I want a computer for Christmas,
With apps, skype and all that's in mode,
I'll program in basic-line graphics,
And I'll try not to let it explode.

****

Wishes build mountains and parents must try
To grant dreams that tower to the sky,
Pounds run to little, they don't understand
As you scrimp and you slave, they demand.

But somewhere tonight, as darkness draws neigh,
A child whimpers and others will cry,
Not for dolls or computers or trainer-shod feet,
But for comfort and something to eat.

****

"Oh send me a meal just for Christmas,
Tasty meat, rice and some bread,
Soup or some cheese, potatoes or peas,
And a place I can rest a tired head."

"Oh send me a shelter for Christmas,
From where I need never roam,
Where no hunger is found, with walls that are sound,
A place that a child can call home."

"Oh send me some love just for Christmas,
Let me learn how to smile for one day,
Let hunger be gone, let us all be as one,
Let troubles and fear fade away."

****

Children write lists for one thing or another,
One wants a computer, one just wants a mother,
Some hands will be filled, some bellies will not,
Some will be remembered, some will be forgot,
And Christmas will come, and Christmas will go,
For some sun will shine, for some wind will blow,
But out there a child waits, with hope and a prayer,
For the Christmas to come,
when the world learns to care.

~ SANTA CLAUS ~

They hung him on the Christmas Tree
with a string around his throat,
his face was bright and shiny
like the buttons on his coat.

He'd a buckle on his belly,
and boots up to the knee,
and when no-one was looking
he'd spin around with glee.

But he was made of chocolate
such a tempting, tasty treat,
so that Johnny went and ate him
from his bonnet to his feet.

~ UNDER AN EAGLE'S WING ~

Great feathered wings soar ever high
Against a star-besprinkled sky,
Whilst drifting softly down below
Where streams and gentle rivers flow,
Christmas in her glory falls
On sleeping hills and dry stone walls,
Smoke spirals on the frosted air,
Children ask, "Is Santa there?"
Trees in silver raiment wait
For carol singers round the gate
And age old melodies they sing -
Underneath an Eagle's wing.

Through cloud and mist or golden dawn
As on that day The Child was born,
Whilst puddings boil and turkeys roast
And glasses are upraised in Toast,
Past mist-clad mountains, mirrored lakes,
Through rock-strewn ridges white with flakes.
Whilst Christians gathering far below
Share love and dreams with those they know,
A bird flies by to blessings bring
To those beneath an Eagle's Wing.

THE WONDER

It's the wonder of it all -

To a stall or cave, of smells and straw
unlit, unfit for anything but beasts
they came. The woman cumbersome with pain,
the man desperate, angry and afraid.
He laid her best he could on straw,
searching for some dry,
while she would cry
and try to think of angels.

Minutes limped, he held her hand,
unplanned this makeshift bed,
perhaps he stroked her hair
wet with un-dried sweat
helpless in his fear, her time grew near,
there in the lonely gloom,
they prayed it would be over soon.

A final push, a gush of life
all slime and blood, a cry to show He breathed.
Relieved, they cleaned around
found fresh straw,
placed the baby at the breast
and rested in that stall -
That was the wonder of it all.

~ JACK FROST ~

Jack Frost with fingers white
Came to visit us last night,
Mist he left upon the glass
That we might know, that he did pass.

I tried to rub the rime away
To look upon the crisp new day,
But my scraping was in vain
Crusted is my window pane.

Hear the crackling of the grass
Crunching as my footsteps pass,
And all the trees are hung with lace
Sparkling garlands every place.

Perhaps the sun may come to call,
To warm us up, and melt it all,
But old Jack Frost skips on his way
To come again another day.

WHAT IS CHRISTMAS?

They asked me. "What is Christmas?"
But no answer could I find,
Is it tinselled cards and mistletoe,
Or, 'Peace to all mankind'?
Is it angel-wings and candlelight,
Or choirboys round a tree,
Frankincense and gold and myrrh,
Wise Men one, two, three?

Perhaps it's parcels tied with ribbon,
Or a bright star in the night,
Roof-tops clad in morning snow
With grey streets dressed in white?
Perhaps it's shepherds on the hillsides,
Santa on his sleigh,
Chimney-pots and children's smiles
A donkey in the hay?

Perhaps it's the love in some hearts
A small child left behind -
But when they asked me. "What is Christmas?"
No answer could I find.

~ THE DONKEY ~

"Who were they?" The donkey asked,
as he rested in his stall.
"Voices hushed, they crept inside,
then shrank against the wall,
Marvel filled their faces, they clutched their staffs with fear,
'Till the woman beckoned with her hand,
and called them to draw near."

Plain men from off the hills they were,
honest and unspoiled,
With little value in their hands,
for all the hours they toiled,
Suddenly the night was bright,
and nothing was the same
Their lives were thrown in turmoil,
that night the Angels came.

"Who were they?" the donkey asked,
munching on his hay.
"Great men who walked with dignity,
they came from far away,
Splendid robes, guided crowns, they entered in with ease,
Then - humbled by a tiny babe, they fell upon their knees."

Precious gifts upon the straw, frankincense and gold,
Myrrh the gift of pain and tears and so it was foretold -
The story never changing, shines forever bright,
But no-one asked the donkey, what he saw that night.

~ CHRISTMAS PRESENTS AND THE JOY OF CHRISTMAS SHOPPING!!! ~

I'm sorting out 'me presents,
    Now - lets see what I've got,
Isn't it a nightmare
    Deciding who gets what?

I've got these fancy notelets
Of a lovely Persian cat,
Aunty Mabel writes a lot
I think I'll send her that.
Oh! But wait a minute
I know she can't stand those,
Cats bring her out in pimples
And their fur gets up her nose.
    If I send them cousin Lizzy
    She'll just shove 'em on a shelf,
    She never even sends a card -
    Oh - I'll keep them for me'self.

Now who will have this bubble bath?
Pew! It has an awful pong,
Perhaps for my posh aunty -
Oh no, that would be wrong,
She only shops in Harrods
    This would never pass the test,
    I'll send a box of hankies,
    Perhaps that would be best.

I've a calendar for Canada,
Of course it's W.I.
For that lady, now what was her name?
I'll remember if I try.
I met her once in Kendal,
Or was it on a train?
She had a blue-rinse hair-do
Now, what was her name?
She always sends a lovely card,
Last year she sent some soap,
Which smelt like rotting cabbage,
Suspended on a rope,
I kept it in the garden shed,
I'm sure it's very green,
It'll do for Aunty Bertha -
She'll not know where it's been.

> I've a scarf for Mrs. Perkins
> To keep her warm in bed,
> I send her one each Christmas -
> Hang on! The old girl's dead!!

Then, I've woolly gloves for Sharon,
I wonder if they'll fit?
She's got fingers like bananas
And I've purled, instead of knit!
I don't think she'll notice,
It'll show her that I care,
It doesn't really matter
That they're not a perfect pair.

Then I've socks for Uncle Henry,
And socks for Uncle Mike,
And socks for Jim and Tommy,
For Fred, and Dave and Spike.
I've a nice pair for the Vicar
With squiggles round about,
And another pair for Eddie,
Well - that's the men all sorted out!

Who will have this five year diary?
What's this supposed to be?
I bought it at the Chapel Sale
For twenty seven p.
    There's this tin of talcum powder
    That'll do for Mrs. Kerr,
    And this pretty box of bath cubes -
    No, she sent me them last year!

I've rushed round Marks and Spenser's,
Splashed through puddles in the rain,
Battled scowling shop assistants,
Vowed, "I won't go there again!!"
I've been round and round the market,
'Till me feet and nerves were frayed,
    I'd nothing in me purse but fluff
    When all the bills were paid.

But - I've made a resolution,
That it's really got to end,
There must be more to Christmas
Than SHOP and TRAMP and SPEND!

So to save me nervous breakdown,
And before I'm quite worn out,
Next year I'm going to treat myself,
And send everybody - **'NOWT!!'**

CHRISTMAS SKY

Beneath a Christmas sky
Where robin and the raven fly,
Cruising clouds in silence sail
Washing towns and lonely vale.

Down below we scurry on our way,
Shopping, wrapping, baking for The Day,
As if a siege or famine were to come,
Not the birth of God's own Son.

Sing your carols, fill your lives with joy,
Remembering it's about a new-born boy,
Who lights our lives as they sweep by,
Underneath a Christmas sky.

THE DREAM

In the silence of the stars
I dreamed a dream of angels singing,
from the East the Magi came
presents to a new King bringing,
while a mother nursed her child
amidst the tumbling straw and glory,
shepherds crowded through the door
sharing in the timeless story.

Then the moment fled away
leaving nothing as it seemed,
just a breathless hush remained,
waiting in the dream I dreamed.

EIGHTY FIVE CHRISTMAS'S

(To commemorate 85th Anniversary of Cumbria Westmorland W.I. in 2005)

Eighty five Christmas's flowing away
Snow on the fell-tops,
Bells on a sleigh,
Friendship and laughter, carols to sing,
Flowers round a cradle,
Gifts for The King,
Millions of meetings, parties to plan,
Mince-pies and music,
And cakes by the van!
Journeys to London, theatres and views,
Fighting for freedom,
Making The News.

Facing the future with courage and care,
Making men realise
That women are there
Not just for cooking with children to rear,
But for thinking and shaping
A world without fear.
Preserving our history, proud to achieve,
Passing on talents
Because we believe
Not just in the values, the past sends our way
But in doing the best we can
Day after day.

So, join in the singing, and hold your heads high,
        Women together
                The W. I.
Eighty five Christmas's, let the words soar,
        Onwards and upwards,
                For eighty five more.

~ THROUGH THE CHRISTMAS WINDOW ~

In through the Christmas window
see a fir-tree's twinkling lights,
hung with silver bells and baubles,
dressed with many sweet delights,
see the multi-coloured parcels,
a table weighed with fare,
hear the crackers pulled and popping,
and the laughter that we share.

Out through the Christmas window,
friends and family come to call,
welcomed in with hugs and kisses,
"Merry Christmas to you all."
By streaks of winter sunshine,
watch a robin in the snow,
I think back on other Christmas's
we shared so long ago.

But – through the special window,
behold the Three Wise Men,
and a group of humble shepherds
on their way to Bethlehem.
See a woman tend a baby
as he gurgles in the hay,
a tiny child named Jesus,
who will save the world one day.

~ WINTER ~

Silence beneath a starry sky,
iced fingers dressing tiles,
etching patterns on cold glass,
passing over grass, unearthly spectre,
stroking path and yard,
soft soil turned hard,
pointed daggers drip.

Tormented winds howl,
gather force,
tearing trees,
bringing structures
to their knees.
Black sheeting rain
dashes down,
hour on hour
to flood the fields
burst river banks,
and make them yield.

Nature laughs,
revelling,
in its power.

THE CHRISTMAS HAPPY SONG

Christmas jing-a-ling, Christmas ting-a-ling,
The Christmas Happy Song,
Children sing-a-ling, church bells ring-a-ding,
Ring-a-ding all day long.

Angels one, two, three,
On the Christmas Tree,
Sweetly sing for you,
Robins round your head,
Presents on the bed,
All your dreams come true.

Out into the snow,
Wrapped up warm we go,
Smiles on every face,
It's a holiday,
Laughter for today,
Join the snowball chase,

Santa's on his way,
With his loaded sleigh,
Dashing past the moon,
Bringing love and joy,
To each girl and boy,
He'll be with you soon.

Christmas jing-a-ling, Christmas ting-a-ling,
The Christmas Happy Song,
Children sing-a-ling, church bells ring-a-ding,
Ring-a-ding all day long.

CHRISTMAS IN THE VILLAGE

There's Christmas in the air, so we prepare.
The village tree appears, in twinkling tiers,
the festive glow is shared, by other trees,
window lights and trim, inviting friends 'Come In,'
as plans are laid for feasts and fun.

Busy Herald 'The Christmas Farmers Market'
packed with people, stacked with food and gifts.
While up in Church, Bell Ringers chime,
the Choir sings sweet in festive rhyme.

As Santa's reindeer days dash by,
until at last it's Christmas Eve,
when local carol singers weave
their lilting passage home by home,
voices echo as they roam,
through storm and squall,
or swirling snow, joy walks with them
as they go.

Blessed Christmas morning dawns,
with children's squeals, and parents yawns,
the church resounds with song and psalm,
while in the village all is calm.
Inside our small cocoon we bide,
the perilous world is left outside,
but when is stilled the Christmas song,
the village will still drift along.

NO ROOM AT THE INN

The church bells rang one Christmas Eve
With snowflakes sprinkling down,
The wind was shrieking through the streets
When a beggar boy entered town.
He'd a threadless shirt round his shoulders,
And nothing but snow for his feet,
Shivering, desperate and starving,
He shook as he limped down the street.
He wanted just a night's shelter,
Maybe a crust of bread,
He'd searched all day for refuge,
But he'd reached the night unfed.
His strength was slowly failing,
He could go no more that night,
He sank upon a door-step,
When upon him shone a light.
An Inn-door nearby was opened,
By a grease-fat man with a stick,
He frowned down at the vagrant child,
Then gave the lad a kick.
"Move on! Get out! There's no place for you!"
"Be off! Get out of here!"
The child got up and crawled away
Into a world of fear.
Christmas day awoke on earth,
A day that should banish all sin,
But on Christmas Eve a small child died,
There was no room at the Inn.

~ A REMEMBER CHRISTMAS ~

Let's have a 'Remember Christmas'
With expectation a-glow,
Waiting for Father Christmas,
Watching the sky for snow,
The round of Yuletide parties,
Jelly and musical chairs,
The crackle of wrapping paper,
As Santa creeps up the stairs.
Those special Christmas mornings
All loving warmth and joy,
The smell of the chicken cooking,
Delight in a new doll or toy.

Through the mists of time I see her
That child by the back-street door,
But if only she could recapture
A 'Remember Christmas' once more.

~ THE COLOURS OF CHRISTMAS ~

Mix green upon the pallet
For the holly and the tree,
Add red for Santa's flowing robe
With a child upon his knee.

Introduce the purest blue,
For The Mother's gown
Which nestles on a bed of straw
By a mangers wooden brown.

Mingle white for angel wings,
Gentle fleece and snow,
Don't forget bright silver,
To make the new star glow.

Finally add a brush of gold,
Which a king brought to a stall.
These the Christmas colours,
Bringing blessings to us all.

NOVEMBER and DECEMBER 2010

Snow bound.
Mound on humped-up mound,
rifts of banked up snow
grow, as if up-rooted from the ground
not fallen from a laden sky
to fly and fall in fleecy beds
upon our heads.

Strange footprints trace the snow
and go in circles
plodding round the hidden ground.
My boots tread slippery pop-corn,
struggling step by step,
any inept move around
could send me tumbling down.

Splendid in a cool and lofty way
is this display of nature's fall
which swaddles all,
disguises post and gate,
bespangles trees in state,
brings the ways of man to heel.

Sealed within our homes
we wait
for the melt, or rain,
when we can move
and live again.

THE CHRISTMAS TREE

He bathed in golden mornings,
and nights of shivering snow,
branches tossed by battering gale,
as seasons spun he stretched up
from the earth below.

He longed to be a special tree,
to quit the forest floor and find
new places where the birds had flown,
leave his tedious home behind.

One day, the woodmen came with saws and trucks,
and though he suffered pain when toppled to the earth,
excitement bubbled in each leaf and bough,
because he thought this was not death but birth.

Carried over sprawling miles,
borne into a Stately Hall,
dressed in the finest fruit and filigree,
with a tinsel star winking down on all,

he knew at last he'd found what perfect bliss could be,
his happiness as children danced around
exploded, as they said how wonderful he was
a Christmas Tree, in splendour gowned.

Inside he trembled, wondering what adventures would be next,
would he be planted proud within a garden or a park?
But cruel hands just tore his finery away
and plunged him lonely in a Box Room in the dark.

Endless days of empty cold, with only mice and rats,
he longed to feel the golden sun again,
he remembered rustling winds on winter days,
he pined to feel the soothing wash of autumn rain.

Dragged from the dark one day, brittle, bare and old,
at last he saw the sky for which he'd yearned,
he thought how happy he had been to be a Christmas Tree,
and with these thoughts he quietly burned.

*(As a child, mum read me The Fir Tree, by Hans Christian Anderson,
because of this, I've only ever had artificial Christmas Trees.)*

CHRISTMAS 1975 and 2015

That first Christmas at The Mill
you filled my bowl with apple pie
tinned custard and delight,
you made that night so special,
and when the Carol Singers came
they stood around the porch
lit by the gentle lamp light beam.
You held me close beneath the glow,
so everyone would know
that we were one.

The Carol Singers came again
this Christmas Eve,
lit by the lamp light beam,
braving damp and rain
they lilted 'Silent Night',
I listened, arms wrapped
round, against the cold,
to the age old tune,
wet faces shone.
Alone I gripped my tears,
for you are gone.

~ AFTER CHRISTMAS ~

Throw out the Christmas Tree
        It's time is done.
One by one, pull down
        The smiling clown, the wingless angel,
The dusty fairy with her yellow locks,
        Push them all back in their box.

Burn this year's decorations
        Now the celebrations past,
They're not supposed to last through
        To another year.
You can buy some more,
Or store them from a New Year sale,
        Unlike, "Goodwill to Men,"
They won't turn stale.

Heap the bath-cubes and the soap
        And hope you grow to like the smell
Of the shower-gel and scent
        Which were kindly meant,
And after all you sent the same -
        It's all part of the Christmas Game.

~ CHRISTMAS MONOLOGUE ~

'Do come in Mrs. Shufflebottom, it's so nice you could join us for Christmas Dinner.

Oh - Penelope - what a pretty name.

Do take your coat off, and get comfy.

Oh, you feel the cold, well we'll just stoke up the Rayburn. Of-course you can keep your coat on for the present, and your hat, and scarf and gloves.

You do feel the cold, don't you?

Pity your husband couldn't join us, you being new to the village.

Oh he's confined. To bed?

Strangeways! I'm sure it was a misunderstanding. Well it's true they don't like people mentioning bombs in airports these days, even if he was joking. He must have a strange sense of humour, but they are touchy. Let's hope he's home soon - he must be a real brick!

No dear, a brick, the type you build houses with, nothing to do with needles.

How did you spend Christmas last year? At a soup kitchen. Well, we can all go through hard times. Oh, you were helping serve, very commendable. I'm sure you got lots of thanks.

You got nits. Me mother always used to swear by Sulio!

Now then, would you like a little melon to start?

Indigestion, since you had your gall bladder out.

Perhaps you'd prefer some prawns. No good since you had everything taken away - you must be really empty in there.

Perhaps just some soup then - you saw enough of that last year.

We best skip onto the main course -we've got a nice big turkey.

You're vegetarian. It's becoming very popular these days. Personally I love me meat and two veg.

How about some Brussels sprouts? You had a bad experience in Brussels. I wouldn't have thought that had anything to do with the sprouts. They give you flatulence, perhaps we better give them a miss.

How about a bit of mash, well I'm glad to see you're eating something, Penelope. Are you sure you can manage in your gloves?

Shall we have some sherry ready for The Queen. No dear, not the pop group, the one with the crown.

You do like your sherry don't you? A little more? Well, I'll let you keep the bottle.

Dear me you have got bad hiccups, shall I get a paper bag? The paper bag was for the hiccups, I didn't really expect you to sick back your mash. Perhaps you should have stuck to soup after all.

Do you think you could squeeze in a little Christmas Pudding, if your stomach's settled? Oh you like Christmas Pudding - that's a relief. Custard? Reminds you of baby's poo - what a vivid imagination you do have.

Just a little white sauce then - oh dear, I think your scarves dropped in it.

You are turning a funny colour Penelope. You cough and I'll bang your back. I think it could be one of those five pence pieces I put in, it must have got stuck.

Eddie, you keep banging her on the back, while I phone the ambulance – she's only coughed up 10p, she owes me 15p!

THE THREE TREES

An oak, an elm and a waving fir
sang 'neath a summer sky.
"What will you be," asked the southern wind,
"when the axe-man chances by?"

"I'll be a ship," said the oak with pride,
"and surge through a stormy sea,
sailors will know that I'm safe and strong
and put their trust in me."

"I'll be the love in a craftsman's hands,"
said the elm, "as he shapes with care
my sturdy wood into faithful friends,
a cupboard or a chair."

But the fir remembered a gypsy babe
she'd rocked in a gentle arm,
stilled his cries through a winter's night
and guarded him from harm.

"I'll be a cradle," the fir tree said,
"and rock to a baby's sighs,
sharing dreams, soothing fear,
watched by an angel's eyes."

So the axe-man came and felled the trees,
with a Chop! Chop! Chop! They fell,
but would their wishes for afterlife
come true? Only fate would tell.

The oak was made into three fine ships,
that sailed on a Christmas morn,
bearing tidings to all the world,
that a precious child was born.

The elm became a comfy chair
where a Story-Teller spun
his tales of timeless magic,
bringing joy to everyone.

But the toppled fir with its knotted grain
became just a box of pine,
left in a stable filled with straw
for ox and ass to dine,
until the night when a carpenter
and his dear wife came to call,
when the fir-tree manger proved to be
the finest tree of all.

(Inspired by a story told by Story-Teller, Taffy Thomas, in Orton Market Hall, Christmas 2005)

THOUGHTS ON NEW YEAR'S EVE

Let us drink to New Year's passed
when the wine flowed free,
raise your glasses high
to the people we used to be,
sing 'till the rafters ring,
open the waiting door,
spare your tears through the passing years
for the friends you'll see no more.

Pause for a fleeting breath
as the chimes of midnight sound,
look back, if you must remember,
be still as you look around,
but walk not alone, with shadows
they are gone with the mist of time
to leave but a blurring memory,
which becomes my New Year rhyme.

So, fill your glass for tomorrow
clean as the un-trod snow,
unknown, untouched, undamaged,
with a million ways to go.
Tick by tick, the old year's waning,
whether you laugh or mourn,
relentless seconds slip away,
to herald a New Year's dawn.

Jesus is not just for Christmas
He came for a life not a day,
When the tinsel and trimmings
Are back in their box
We shouldn't pack Jesus away.